the
super bowl
50 Pleasing Pastas

Printed in the United States of America
by G&R Publishing Co.

Distributed By:

507 Industrial Street
Waverly, IA 50677

ISBN-13: 978-1-56383-293-2
ISBN-10: 1-56383-293-3
Item # 3613

Table of Contents

Pasta Pointers

Pasta may be purchased in a wide variety of styles.

Shapes

The smallest shapes, like alphabet and ring
pastas, can also be called Soup Pasta.

bow tie (farfalle)   *wheels (rotelle)*   *spirals (rotini)*

corkscrew (cavatappi)   *shells (conchiglie)*   *alphabet*   *rings*

Long Round

These are sometimes called Strand Pastas.

spaghetti   *thin spaghetti*   *vermicelli*   *angel hair (capelli d' angelo)*

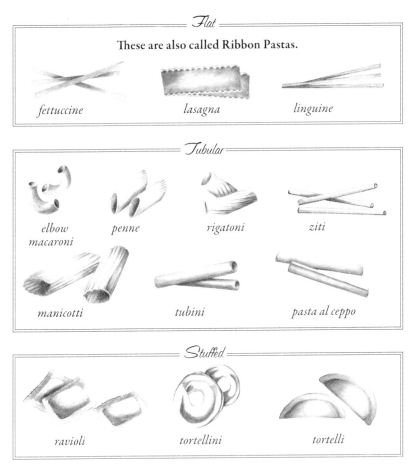

Flat

These are also called Ribbon Pastas.

fettuccine

lasagna

linguine

Tubular

elbow macaroni

penne

rigatoni

ziti

manicotti

tubini

pasta al ceppo

Stuffed

ravioli

tortellini

tortelli

Pasta & Sauces

- Pair thin pastas, such as angel hair, vermicelli or thin spaghetti, with sauces that are light and thin, such as broths, light tomato sauces, and butter or oil-based sauces.

- Thicker pastas, such as fettuccine, pair well with heavier sauces, such as creamy Alfredo sauce.

- Pasta tubes and shapes with curves, twists, ridges or folds are wonderful with chunky sauces, including those with meat.

Pasta may be purchased dried, fresh or frozen

- **Dried pasta** should be stored in airtight containers in a dry, cool area. It can be stored for a long time, but use the expiration date on each package as a guide to freshness.

- **Fresh pasta** is perishable and must be stored in the refrigerator. If not used within 3 or 4 days, it can be frozen for up to a month.

- **Filled pastas,** like ravioli and tortellini, can be found in the refrigerated or frozen food sections of your grocery store.

- If substituting different pasta shapes in any of the recipes, follow the cooking times listed on the package.

- If substituting fresh pasta for dried pasta, reduce cooking times according to package instructions and use about 50% more of the fresh; dried pasta absorbs more water so it swells more when cooked.

- *Unless otherwise noted, recipes in this book use dried pasta.*

Serving Sizes

- According to the USDA, ½ cup of cooked pasta equals one serving of grains. When adding sauces and other ingredients to combination pasta dishes, the size of one serving of the prepared dish will increase.

- For labeling and food preparation purposes, it's recommended to prepare about 2 ounces of dry uncooked pasta (or 1 cup of cooked pasta) per serving for a main dish. This would count as 2 servings of the grain group using USDA guidelines.

- Allow approximately 1 ounce of uncooked pasta per person for most side dishes.

Nutrition Tips

- One way to create a protein-rich meal on a budget is to pair pasta with beans, lentils or low-fat dairy products.

- For low-fat sauces, use a base made from broth or pureed vegetables in place of cream or butter. Add spices and fresh herbs for flavor and texture.

- Use a combination of low-fat or no-fat mayonnaise with real mayonnaise to reduce calories. You can also thin creamy dressings with a little skim milk for a smooth blend with the pasta.

Pointers for Cooking Pasta

- Use plenty of water in a large pot, but don't overfill it or the water will boil over. Three quarts of water is enough to cook 4 to 8 ounces of pasta. This will allow pasta to move freely and cook without sticking together or to the bottom of the pan.

- Adjust the quantity of water accordingly when cooking larger quantities of pasta. For example, to cook a pound of pasta, fill a 6- to 8-quart pot about ¾ full of water.

- When the water begins to boil, add a small amount of salt and allow it to dissolve before pasta is added. Salted water improves the natural flavor of the pasta.

- Don't add oil to the cooking water if you plan to serve the pasta with sauce. Although oil prevents pasta from sticking together, the pieces will become slippery and sauce will not cling well.

- Dry pasta takes longer to cook than fresh pasta so follow package instructions for best results.

- Pasta should be cooked **al dente** (al DEN tay). In Italian, this means "to the tooth". Pasta cooked al dente is tender, yet firm; it's not soft or overdone. The pasta is tender on the outside but gives a slight resistance when cut with a fork or chewed because the core of the pasta is partly uncooked.

- Pasta is close to being done when it is slightly swollen and begins to rise toward the top of the water. Then it's time to check the tenderness.

- If adding cooked pasta to a dish that will be baked in an oven for more than 30 minutes, shorten the boiling time to avoid mushy pasta. Cook it for ½ to ⅔ of the normal cooking time directed on the package before adding it to the casserole dish.

- Pasta continues to cook when it's drained so sauces should be added quickly and the hot pasta should be served promptly.

- If pasta will be reheated later, toss it with a bit of olive oil and refrigerate in an airtight container. Before serving, place pasta in boiling water for 1 minute, drain and serve.

To rinse or not to rinse . . .

- Don't rinse pasta which will be served warm with sauce; the starchy residue on the warm cooked pasta helps bind the sauce to it.

- For pasta which will be used in cold salads, the quickest method to chill the pasta is to place it in a colander and thoroughly rinse it in cold water to chill it immediately. But if time allows, it's better to rinse the cooked pasta only briefly in cold water, put the salad together while the pasta is still slightly warm and then chill the entire salad in the refrigerator until serving time. The reason? Warm pasta absorbs salad dressing better than cold pasta, so flavors will be better if the dressing is added when the pasta is still somewhat warm.

All-American
BBQ Beef and Noodles

Makes 6 servings

Ingredients

*12 oz. uncooked rigatoni
or ziti pasta*

1 T. vegetable oil

1 onion, finely sliced

2 T. Worcestershire sauce

1 lb. lean ground beef

3 to 4 T. barbeque sauce

*1 (14.5 oz.) can crushed
tomatoes, undrained*

Salt

*4 to 6 drops hot pepper
sauce, optional*

Directions

In a large saucepan over medium-high heat, bring lightly salted water to a boil. Add pasta to water, stir and return to a boil. Cook uncovered for 12 to 15 minutes or to desired doneness, stirring occasionally. Meanwhile, heat the oil in a large skillet over medium-high heat. Add the onion and sauté about 1 minute. Reduce heat to medium, add Worcestershire sauce and cover the skillet. Cook until onion is tender, about 4 to 5 minutes. Uncover the skillet and add the beef; cook until meat is crumbly and no longer pink. Add the barbeque sauce and crushed tomatoes with juice. Simmer until mixture is hot, stirring occasionally. Season with salt and pepper sauce to taste. When pasta is tender, drain well and divide it among six serving bowls. Spoon the sauce over each portion and serve immediately.

Pasta Con Carne

Makes 6 to 8 servings

Ingredients

12 to 16 oz. uncooked rotini
   or bow tie pasta

1 lb. lean ground beef

1 medium onion, chopped

1 (15 oz.) can tomato sauce

1 (8 oz.) jar taco sauce

1 C. canned kidney or pinto
   beans, rinsed and drained

1 tsp. chili powder

1 tsp. butter

¾ C. shredded Cheddar cheese

½ C. low-fat sour cream

Directions

In a large saucepan over medium-high heat, bring lightly salted water to a boil. Add pasta to water, stir and return to a boil. Cook uncovered for 8 to 12 minutes or to desired doneness, stirring occasionally. Meanwhile, in a large saucepan over medium heat, brown ground beef with onion until meat is cooked through and onion is tender. Drain off excess fat. Stir in tomato sauce, taco sauce, beans and chili powder. Bring mixture to a boil, reduce heat to low and simmer for 8 minutes, stirring occasionally. When pasta is cooked, drain and toss with butter. Place portions of pasta into individual serving bowls and spoon some of the ground beef mixture on top. Place a dollop of sour cream on top and sprinkle with 2 tablespoons of Cheddar cheese just before serving.

Italian Shell Pasta

Makes 8 servings

Ingredients

2 (14.5 oz.) cans stewed
   tomatoes

2 C. broccoli florets

2 medium carrots,
   thinly sliced

½ tsp. salt

½ tsp. Italian seasoning

½ tsp. dried oregano

¼ tsp. dried basil

4 bacon strips, diced

½ lb. fresh mushrooms, sliced

⅓ C. chopped green bell pepper

¼ C. chopped onion

2 cloves garlic, minced

16 oz. uncooked medium
   shell pasta

1 tsp. butter

¼ C. shredded Parmesan
   cheese

Directions

In a large saucepan over medium-high heat, combine stewed tomatoes, broccoli, carrots, salt, Italian seasoning, oregano and basil. Bring mixture to a boil, reduce heat, cover and simmer for 25 to 30 minutes or until broccoli and carrots are tender. In a medium skillet over medium heat, cook bacon until crisp. Drain bacon on paper towels, reserving 1 tablespoon of drippings in the skillet. In the drippings, sauté the mushrooms, green pepper, onion and garlic until tender. Add mushroom mixture to tomato mixture and heat through. Meanwhile, in a large saucepan over medium-high heat, bring lightly salted water to a boil. Add pasta to water, stir and return to a boil. Cook uncovered for 10 to 13 minutes or to desired doneness, stirring occasionally. Drain pasta and place in a large serving bowl, adding butter and stirring well to coat. Top pasta with vegetable mixture, then sprinkle with bacon and Parmesan cheese. Serve immediately.

Cajun Fettuccine

Makes 3 to 4 servings

Ingredients

8 oz. uncooked fettuccine pasta

1 C. heavy whipping cream
or evaporated fat-free milk

1 tsp. Cajun or Creole
seasoning

1 (7 oz.) jar roasted red bell
peppers, drained

½ lb. fully cooked smoked
sausage, cut in ¼″ slices

2 medium green onions, sliced

Directions

In a large saucepan over medium-high heat, bring lightly salted water to a boil. Add pasta to water, stir and return to a boil. Cook uncovered for 10 to 13 minutes, stirring occasionally. Meanwhile, in a blender or food processor, combine whipping cream, Cajun seasoning and bell peppers. Cover and blend on high speed until smooth. Pour pepper mixture into a large skillet and cook over medium heat, stirring occasionally, until mixture thickens. Reduce heat and stir in sausage. Cook until heated through, but do not boil. Drain fettuccine and place in a large serving bowl. Spoon sausage mixture over pasta and sprinkle with green onions. Serve immediately.

Stir-Fry Oriental Beef over Pasta

Makes 4 servings

Ingredients

12 oz. boneless beef top sirloin steak, partially frozen

4 oz. uncooked spaghetti or vermicelli, broken into pieces

¼ C. orange juice

2 T. hoisin sauce

1 T. reduced-sodium soy sauce

½ tsp. toasted sesame oil

⅛ tsp. cayenne pepper

1 clove garlic, minced

2 C. fresh asparagus pieces

1 medium carrot, cut into thin strips

1 small red onion, cut into wedges

Toasted sesame seeds*, optional

Directions

Trim any fat off beef. Cut beef across the grain into thin strips; set aside. In a large saucepan over medium-high heat, bring lightly salted water to a boil. Add pasta to water, stir and return to a boil. Cook uncovered for 8 to 10 minutes or to desired doneness, stirring occasionally. Drain pasta, cover and keep warm. Meanwhile, in a small bowl, stir together orange juice, hoisin sauce, soy sauce, sesame oil and cayenne pepper; set aside. Spray an unheated wok or large skillet with nonstick cooking spray; preheat over medium-high heat until a drop of water sizzles. Add garlic and stir-fry for 15 seconds. Add asparagus and carrot; stir-fry for 1 minute. Add red onion and stir-fry for 2 to 3 additional minutes or until vegetables are crisp-tender. Remove vegetables from wok or skillet. Add beef to wok or skillet and stir-fry about 3 minutes or to desired doneness. Return vegetables to wok or skillet. Drizzle orange sauce over all and toss to coat ingredients. Cook until heated through. Place prepared pasta into individual serving bowls and spoon meat mixture over pasta. Garnish with a sprinkling of toasted sesame seeds, if desired.

To toast, place sesame seeds in a single layer on a baking sheet. Bake at 350° for approximately 10 minutes or until sesame seeds are golden brown.

Mexican Pasta Wheels

Makes 6 to 8 servings

Ingredients

2 tsp. vegetable oil
1 C. chopped onion
1 tsp. ground cumin
1 tsp. chili powder
1 tsp. minced garlic
1 lb. lean ground beef
1 tsp. salt

6 C. chopped fresh
   plum tomatoes
16 oz. uncooked rotelle pasta
1 C. shredded pepper
   jack cheese
1½ C. tortilla chips, broken
¼ C. sliced green onions

Directions

Heat the oil in a large skillet over medium-high heat. Add onion and cook until tender, about 5 minutes. Stir in cumin, chili powder and garlic; cook for 30 seconds. Add ground beef and salt; cook until browned, stirring occasionally. Stir in tomatoes and cook for 5 minutes or until softened. Meanwhile, in a large saucepan over medium-high heat, bring lightly salted water to a boil. Add pasta to water, stir and return to a boil. Cook uncovered for 9 to 12 minutes or to desired doneness, stirring occasionally. Drain pasta, then toss with sauce and cheese. Transfer pasta to individual serving bowls and top each serving with ¼ cup tortilla chips and about 2 teaspoons of green onions.

Creamy Mac and Ham

Makes 4 to 6 servings

Ingredients

12 oz. uncooked elbow
  macaroni pasta

½ lb. fresh mushrooms

2 T. butter

1 tsp. caraway seeds

½ lb. smoked, diced ham

⅔ C. sour cream

¼ C. fresh grated
  Parmesan cheese

Salt and pepper

Garlic powder

Butter sprinkles, optional

Directions

In a large saucepan over medium-high heat, bring lightly salted water to a boil. Add pasta to water, stir and return to a boil. Cook uncovered for 7 to 10 minutes or to desired doneness, stirring occasionally. Meanwhile, remove the mushroom stems, wipe the caps clean with a damp paper towel and cut the caps into thin slices. Melt the butter in a medium saucepan over medium heat. Add the mushrooms and sauté until tender, about 3 minutes. Add the caraway seeds and ham; continue to sauté for 3 more minutes or until ham is heated through; set aside. Drain cooked pasta and place into a large serving bowl. Add the sour cream, Parmesan cheese and ham mixture, tossing until thoroughly mixed. Season to taste with salt, pepper, garlic powder and optional butter sprinkles. Serve immediately.

Peppery Shrimp Alfredo

Makes 4 servings

Ingredients

8 oz. uncooked penne pasta

¼ C. butter

2 T. extra-virgin olive oil

1 onion, diced

2 cloves garlic, minced

1 red bell pepper, seeded and diced

½ lb. portobello mushrooms, diced

1 lb. medium shrimp, peeled and deveined

1 (16 oz.) jar prepared Alfredo sauce

½ C. grated Romano cheese

½ C. heavy cream or half 'n half

1 tsp. cayenne pepper or to taste

Salt and pepper

¼ C. chopped fresh parsley

Directions

In a large saucepan over medium-high heat, bring lightly salted water to a boil. Add pasta to water, stir and return to a boil. Cook uncovered for 10 to 13 minutes or to desired doneness, stirring occasionally. Drain pasta and keep warm in pan. Meanwhile, in a medium saucepan over medium heat, melt the butter with the olive oil. Stir in onion and cook until tender and translucent, about 2 minutes. Stir in garlic, red pepper and mushrooms; cook over medium-high heat until soft, about 2 additional minutes. Stir in the shrimp and cook until firm and pink. Add Alfredo sauce, Romano cheese and cream. Heat to a simmer and cook about 5 minutes or until thickened, stirring constantly. Stir in cayenne pepper; season with salt and pepper to taste. Stir warm pasta into the sauce, transfer to a serving bowl and sprinkle chopped parsley on top. Serve immediately.

Dilled Salmon Pasta

Makes 3 to 4 servings

Ingredients

2 C. uncooked rotini pasta

¼ C. dry white wine

Juice from 1 lemon

¾ lb. salmon fillets,
  bones removed

⅓ C. mayonnaise

3 T. buttermilk

2 tsp. prepared horseradish

1 tsp. dried dillweed

2 tsp. chopped fresh chives or
  ½ tsp. dried minced onion

1 clove garlic, minced

1 small cucumber, peeled
  and diced, optional

Salt and pepper

Directions

In a large saucepan over medium-high heat, bring lightly salted water to a boil. Add pasta to water, stir and return to a boil. Cook uncovered for 8 to 10 minutes or to desired doneness, stirring occasionally. Meanwhile, in a large skillet over high heat, stir together the wine, lemon juice and ¼ cup water. Bring mixture to a simmer, then reduce heat to low. Place salmon in the liquid and simmer for 5 to 10 minutes or just until cooked through, turning once. Turn off the heat and let salmon rest in the liquid for 10 minutes. In a small bowl, whisk together the mayonnaise, buttermilk, horseradish, dillweed, chives and garlic until well blended. Drain pasta and transfer to a medium serving bowl. Break salmon into chunks and remove from liquid; add to pasta. Stir in optional cucumber pieces. Pour dressing on ingredients in bowl and toss gently, adding salt and pepper to taste. Serve immediately. Any leftover salad can be refrigerated and eaten chilled.

Jerk Chicken Pineapple Pasta

Makes 4 servings

Ingredients

4 oz. uncooked fettuccini noodles

1 T. extra-virgin olive oil

2 skinless boneless chicken breast halves, cubed

1 (8 oz.) can pineapple tidbits with juice

¼ C. flaked coconut

2 T. brown sugar

1 tsp. jerk seasoning

½ tsp. ground cinnamon

½ tsp. chili powder

½ tsp. crushed red pepper flakes

Salt and pepper

Directions

In a large saucepan over medium-high heat, bring lightly salted water to a boil. Add pasta to water, stir and return to a boil. Cook uncovered for 10 to 13 minutes or to desired doneness, stirring occasionally. Meanwhile, heat olive oil in a large skillet over medium heat. Add chicken and cook, stirring occasionally, until chicken is no longer pink and juices run clear, 7 to 10 minutes. Stir in pineapple with juice, coconut, brown sugar, jerk seasoning, cinnamon, chili powder and red pepper flakes. Season with salt and pepper to taste. Reduce heat to low and simmer mixture for 15 minutes. When pasta is done, drain and set aside to keep warm. Place chicken mixture in a large serving bowl, add pasta and toss well. Serve immediately.

Fajita Chicken Pasta

Makes 6 to 8 servings

Ingredients

12 oz. uncooked egg noodles

1 (8 oz.) container sour cream

½ C. chipotle liquid meat
marinade

2 T. lime juice

1 tsp. chili powder

1 tsp. ground cumin

½ tsp. crushed red
pepper flakes

3 T. extra-virgin olive
oil, divided

½ C. chopped onion

1 medium red bell pepper,
seeded and cut into
thin strips

1 fresh Anaheim or other mild
chile pepper*, seeded and cut
into thin strips

3 skinless boneless chicken
breast halves, cut into
thin strips

1 T. snipped fresh cilantro,
optional

Directions

In a large saucepan over medium-high heat, bring lightly salted water to a boil. Add pasta to water, stir and return to a boil. Cook uncovered for 8 to 11 minutes or to desired doneness, stirring occasionally. Drain pasta and keep warm in pan. Meanwhile, in medium bowl, combine sour cream, marinade, lime juice, chili powder, cumin and crushed red pepper; set aside. Heat 1 tablespoon of oil in a large skillet over medium heat. Add onion, red pepper strips and chile pepper; cook 4 to 5 minutes or until vegetables are crisp-tender. Remove vegetables from skillet and set aside. Add 1 tablespoon oil to the same skillet and cook half the chicken for 2 to 3 minutes over medium-high heat or until chicken is no longer pink. Remove from skillet and repeat with remaining tablespoon of oil and remaining chicken. Add cooked chicken, vegetables and sour cream mixture to pasta in saucepan; toss to coat. Heat on low until all ingredients are heated through. Transfer mixture to a serving bowl, garnish with optional cilantro and serve immediately.

Wear gloves when working with chile peppers to avoid burns caused by contact with skin and eyes.

Artichoke and Feta Pasta

Makes 4 to 6 servings

Ingredients

12 oz. uncooked rotini pasta

1 (14 oz.) can artichoke hearts
 packed in water, drained

3 large Roma or other
 plum tomatoes

1 (2.25 oz.) can sliced black
 olives, drained

4 oz. feta cheese, crumbled

⅓ C. extra-virgin olive oil

¼ C. red wine vinegar

½ (0.6 oz.) env. dry Italian
 salad dressing mix

¼ C. chopped fresh parsley

Pepper

Directions

In a large saucepan over medium-high heat, bring lightly salted water to a boil. Add pasta to water, stir and return to a boil. Cook uncovered for 8 to 10 minutes or to desired doneness, stirring occasionally. Meanwhile, chop drained artichokes into bite-size pieces and place in a large mixing bowl. Cut tomatoes into thin strips; add to artichokes in bowl. Add olives, feta cheese, oil, vinegar and Italian dressing mix. Stir until well blended; set aside. When pasta is tender, drain well and add to vegetable mixture. Toss well to mix. Add parsley and season with pepper to taste. Serve immediately.

Rotelle with Roasted Corn and Zucchini

Makes 6 to 8 servings

Ingredients

2 ears fresh corn

16 oz. uncooked rotelle
or rotini pasta

2 tsp. extra-virgin olive oil

2 medium zucchini, chopped

½ C. diced red onion

1 tsp. dried oregano

1 C. reduced-sodium
chicken broth

⅓ C. roasted garlic cloves

2 T. chopped fresh parsley

Salt and pepper

½ C. crumbled feta cheese

Directions

Preheat oven to 400°. Wrap corn in foil and roast in oven for about 1 hour. Remove from oven and let corn cool. (This can be completed in advance.) In a large saucepan over medium-high heat, bring lightly salted water to a boil. Add pasta to water, stir and return to a boil. Cook uncovered for 8 to 10 minutes or to desired doneness, stirring occasionally. Drain, but reserve 1 cup of the cooking water. Transfer pasta to a large bowl. Cut corn kernels off the cob; set aside. Heat the oil in a large skillet over medium heat. Add corn kernels, zucchini and onion; sauté for 3 minutes or until golden brown. Add oregano and cook for 1 minute. Stir in broth and roasted garlic; bring mixture to a simmer. Simmer for 5 minutes. Pour mixture over pasta and toss to combine, adding cooking water as needed to moisten pasta. Fold in parsley and season with salt and pepper to taste. Spoon portions into individual serving bowls and top with feta cheese.

Ziti with Roasted Eggplant and Pesto

Makes 4 servings

Ingredients

1 medium onion, cut
into 8 wedges

2 T. extra-virgin olive
oil, divided

1 medium eggplant, halved
lengthwise

6 oz. uncooked ziti, penne
or rigatoni pasta

⅓ C. prepared Dried
Tomato Pesto*

¼ tsp. pepper

Salt

2 T. crumbled chèvre or feta
cheese, optional

Snipped fresh basil, optional

Directions

Preheat oven to 425°. Place onion wedges in a large shallow baking
pan and brush with 1 tablespoon of oil. Roast in oven for 10 minutes
and stir. Brush cut sides of eggplant with remaining tablespoon of oil
and place in pan with onion, cut sides down. Roast 15 minutes more

or until onion is golden brown and eggplant is tender. Meanwhile, in a large saucepan over medium-high heat, bring lightly salted water to a boil. Add pasta to water, stir and return to a boil. Cook uncovered for 12 to 15 minutes or to desired doneness, stirring occasionally. Drain pasta and place into a large serving bowl. Add prepared pesto and pepper to hot pasta and toss gently to coat well; cover and keep warm. Cut eggplant into ½"-thick slices. Add roasted eggplant and onion to pasta, season with salt to taste and toss well until coated. Top with crumbled cheese and basil, if desired.

*Dried Tomato Pesto

Measure ¾ cup oil-pack dried tomatoes; drain, reserving the oil. Add enough olive oil to the reserved oil to make ½ cup; set aside. In a food processor, combine the tomatoes, ¼ cup pine nuts or slivered almonds, ¼ cup snipped fresh basil, ½ teaspoon salt and 4 teaspoons minced garlic. Cover and process until finely chopped. With machine running, gradually add the reserved oil, processing until smooth. Use pesto in recipes or on cooked pasta. Refrigerate or freeze unused portions. Makes 1 cup pesto.

Asparagus Pasta Primavera

Makes 4 servings

Ingredients

16 thin stalks fresh asparagus

8 oz. uncooked long fusilli
   or ziti pasta

1 T. olive oil

2 tsp. minced garlic

¼ tsp. white pepper

¼ C. dry white wine

¼ tsp. salt

3 small red, orange and/or
   yellow tomatoes, seeded
   and diced

1 T. butter

¼ C. chopped fresh basil

Directions

Snap off and discard woody bases of fresh asparagus; rinse remaining sections. Cut off the tips and set aside. Slice asparagus stalks diagonally into 1″ pieces; set aside. Meanwhile, in a large saucepan over medium-high heat, bring lightly salted water to a boil. Add pasta to water, stir and return to a boil. Cook uncovered for 11 to 14 minutes or to desired doneness, stirring occasionally. Heat oil in a large skillet over medium heat. Add garlic and white pepper; cook and stir for 30 seconds. Add asparagus stalk pieces, wine and salt to skillet. Bring mixture to a boil, reduce heat and cook uncovered for 3 minutes or until asparagus is crisp-tender, stirring occasionally. Add tomatoes and asparagus tips; cook uncovered for 1 additional minute or until the tomatoes are heated through. Remove from heat and stir in butter. Drain water off pasta. Add pasta and basil to vegetables in the skillet. Toss gently to combine. Transfer mixture to a large serving bowl or individual serving bowls. Serve immediately.

Spicy Corn
and Salsa Twists

Makes 4 servings

Ingredients

8 oz. uncooked fusilli
or penne pasta

¼ C. vegetable oil

½ tsp. minced garlic

½ tsp. dried oregano

1 (4 oz.) can chopped
green chiles

2 (10 oz.) pkgs. frozen corn
kernels, thawed

1 (4 oz.) jar sliced pimientos,
drained

¼ to ½ C. prepared salsa

Hot pepper sauce, optional

Directions

In a large saucepan over medium-high heat, bring lightly salted water to a boil. Add pasta to water, stir and return to a boil. Cook uncovered for 11 to 14 minutes or to desired doneness, stirring occasionally. Meanwhile, in a medium saucepan over medium-low heat, combine the vegetable oil, garlic, oregano, green chiles, corn and pimientos. Bring the mixture to a simmer, cover and continue to simmer for about 10 minutes. Drain the cooked pasta and return it to the large saucepan, off the heat. Add the corn sauce and salsa. Sprinkle with hot pepper sauce, if desired, and stir until ingredients are well mixed. Transfer mixture to a large serving bowl and serve immediately.

Hot Cauliflower
and Pasta Toss

Makes 4 servings

Ingredients

*1 head cauliflower, broken
   into florets*

*3 C. uncooked elbow
   macaroni pasta*

*6 T. extra-virgin olive
   oil, divided*

1 clove garlic, minced

1 tsp. crushed red pepper flakes

2 T. minced capers, optional

Salt

*2 to 4 T. chopped fresh basil
   or parsley, optional*

*½ C. grated Parmesan
   or sharp Cheddar cheese*

Directions

Steam the cauliflower until crisp-tender. Cut the cauliflower florets into smaller pieces and set aside. Meanwhile, in a large saucepan over medium-high heat, bring lightly salted water to a boil. Add pasta to water, stir and return to a boil. Cook uncovered for 7 to 10 minutes or to desired doneness, stirring occasionally. About 4 minutes before pasta will be done, heat 4 tablespoons of the oil in a large skillet over medium-high heat. Add the garlic, red pepper flakes and optional capers; sauté until evenly dispersed in oil, about 10 seconds. Add cauliflower pieces and stir-fry mixture until well coated with oil. Cover pan, reduce heat to low and simmer for about 1 minute or until cauliflower is heated through. Season with salt to taste; keep warm in the covered skillet, off the heat. Drain pasta and return to large saucepan, off the heat. Sprinkle pasta with remaining 2 tablespoons of olive oil and toss well. Add cauliflower mixture and optional fresh basil or parsley; toss well. Transfer to a large serving bowl and serve with grated cheese.

For a variation, substitute steamed fresh green beans for the cauliflower and add 1 to 2 tablespoons of tomato paste while stir-frying the vegetables.

St. Louie's Toasted Ravioli

Makes 6 servings

Ingredients

2 T. whole milk

1 egg, slightly beaten

¾ C. Italian seasoned bread crumbs

½ tsp. salt

12 oz. frozen cheese ravioli, thawed

2 C. prepared marinara spaghetti sauce

3 C. vegetable oil for frying

1 T. grated Parmesan cheese

Directions

In a small bowl, whisk together milk and egg. Place bread crumbs and salt in a shallow bowl, stirring to mix well. Dip ravioli pieces into milk mixture and then coat in bread crumbs. In a medium saucepan over medium heat, warm spaghetti sauce until bubbling. Reduce heat to low and continue to simmer. In a large heavy pan, pour oil to a depth of 2″. Heat oil over medium heat until a small amount of breading sizzles and turns brown. Fry ravioli, a few at a time, for 1 minute on each side or until golden. Drain fried ravioli on paper towels. Sprinkle with Parmesan cheese and serve immediately in individual bowls with hot spaghetti sauce.

Portobello Tortellini

Makes 4 to 6 servings

Ingredients

1 (13 oz.) pkg. refrigerated
three-cheese tortellini,
uncooked

3 T. butter

1 clove garlic, minced

2 portobello mushrooms,
chopped

½ lb. button mushrooms,
sliced

¼ C. white wine

1½ tsp. dried basil

Salt and pepper

½ C. grated Parmesan cheese

Directions

In a large saucepan over medium-high heat, bring lightly salted water to a boil. Add pasta to water, stir and return to a boil. Cook uncovered for 8 to 10 minutes or to desired doneness, stirring occasionally. Drain pasta and set aside to keep warm. Meanwhile, in a large skillet over medium heat, melt butter and sauté garlic for 1 minute or until fragrant. Stir in portobello mushrooms, button mushrooms, wine and basil. Season with salt and pepper to taste, cooking until mushrooms are tender. Transfer warm pasta to a serving bowl and fold in mushroom mixture. Top with Parmesan cheese and serve immediately.

Nut -n- Cheese Fettuccine

Makes 4 to 6 servings

Ingredients

*1 (9 oz.) pkg. refrigerated
fettuccine or linguine
pasta, uncooked*

*¾ C. chopped hazelnuts,
pecans and/or pine nuts*

1 T. butter

1 T. extra-virgin olive oil

*½ C. crumbled Gorgonzola
or other blue cheese*

*¼ C. shredded Parmesan
cheese*

2 T. snipped fresh basil

Fresh basil leaves, optional

Directions

In a large saucepan over medium-high heat, bring lightly salted water to a boil. Add pasta to water, stir and return to a boil. Cook uncovered for 1 to 3 minutes or to desired doneness, stirring occasionally. Drain pasta and set aside to keep warm. Meanwhile, in a medium skillet over medium heat, combine butter and olive oil. Cook nuts until toasted and butter begins to brown, stirring frequently. Add nut mixture, Gorgonzola, Parmesan cheese and snipped basil to warm pasta, tossing gently to coat well. Transfer mixture to a serving bowl and garnish with fresh basil leaves, if desired. Serve immediately.

Super Pasta Pointer

Here's a formula for creating your own pasta combinations:
4 C. cooked pasta + 1 lb. meat + 2 C. sauce + 2-4 C.
vegetables + seasonings = tasty pasta dish to serve 4

Angel Hair and Broccoli Toss

Makes 4 to 6 servings

Ingredients

1 (25.5 oz.) jar chunky
garden pasta sauce (with
mushrooms, green pepper
and onion)

1 C. half 'n half

2 cloves garlic, pressed

½ tsp. salt

¼ tsp. pepper

⅛ tsp. ground nutmeg

1 T. dried basil

10 oz. uncooked angel
hair pasta

2 C. broccoli florets

2 T. grated Parmesan cheese

2 T. shredded mozzarella
cheese

Directions

In a large saucepan over low heat, combine pasta sauce, half 'n half, garlic, salt, pepper, nutmeg and basil. Simmer for 45 to 50 minutes but do not boil. In another large saucepan over medium-high heat, bring lightly salted water to a boil. Add pasta to water, stir and return to a boil. Cook uncovered for 5 to 6 minutes or to desired doneness, stirring occasionally. Meanwhile, steam the broccoli until crisp-tender. Cut the cooked broccoli into smaller pieces and set aside. Drain pasta. Place a portion of hot cooked pasta into individual serving bowls. Top with some sauce, then some broccoli. Sprinkle Parmesan and mozzarella cheeses on top and serve immediately.

For variations, substitute cheese tortellini or linguine for the angel hair pasta. Small cooked shrimp can also be added.

Summer Vegetable Pasta Bake

Makes 8 to 10 servings

Ingredients

3 C. fresh green beans,
   diagonally cut into 2″ pieces

2½ C. uncooked bow tie pasta

3 C. thinly sliced yellow
   summer squash

2 T. butter

2 C. sliced fresh mushrooms

½ C. chopped onion

3 T. snipped fresh basil
   or 1 T. dried basil

2 T. snipped fresh oregano
   or 2 tsp. dried oregano

2 T. flour

½ tsp. salt

½ tsp. pepper

2¼ C. milk

½ C. shredded Swiss cheese

1 to 2 T. Dijon mustard

Few drops hot pepper sauce

4 to 6 plum tomatoes,
   diagonally sliced

1 C. soft bread crumbs

¼ C. grated Parmesan cheese

Directions

In a large saucepan over medium-high heat, bring lightly salted water to a boil. Add green beans and return to a boil. Cover loosely and cook for 5 minutes. Add pasta and boil for 5 additional minutes. Add squash and return to a boil for 5 minutes or until vegetables are tender; drain and set aside. Preheat oven to 400°. Meanwhile in a large skillet over medium heat, melt butter. Add mushrooms, onion, basil and oregano and cook until tender. Stir in flour, salt and pepper. Add milk, cooking and stirring until slightly thickened, smooth and bubbly. Reduce heat to low and stir in Swiss cheese, mustard and hot pepper sauce to taste; cook for 1 additional minute. Gently toss cheese mixture with pasta-vegetable mixture. Carefully fold in tomatoes. Spoon mixture into a 3-quart casserole, 9 x 13″ baking dish or individual ramekins. In a small bowl, stir together bread crumbs and Parmesan cheese; sprinkle mixture over casserole. Bake 20 to 25 minutes or until heated through. Serve as a side dish or in individual serving bowls as a main course.

Cheesy Vegetable Bowls

Makes 4 servings

Ingredients

8 oz. uncooked penne pasta

1 T. balsamic vinegar

¾ tsp. salt, divided

4 T. extra-virgin olive oil, divided

2 medium zucchini, cut into chunks

2 medium eggplant, cut into chunks

½ large yellow onion, quartered

2 cloves garlic, minced

½ tsp. dried oregano

4 plum tomatoes, chopped

1 C. prepared pasta sauce

¾ C. crumbled feta cheese

¼ tsp. pepper

½ tsp. crushed red pepper flakes

2 C. shredded mozzarella cheese

Directions

In a large saucepan over medium-high heat, bring lightly salted water to a boil. Add pasta to water, stir and return to a boil. Cook uncovered for 10 to 13 minutes or to desired doneness, stirring occasionally. Drain pasta and set aside to keep warm. Meanwhile, preheat broiler. In a small bowl, whisk together vinegar, ½ teaspoon salt and 1 tablespoon of oil. Place zucchini, eggplant and onion pieces on a broiler pan. Brush with vinegar mixture and broil until tender, about 5 to 8 minutes, turning once. Preheat oven to 350°. In a large saucepan over low heat, combine the garlic and remaining 3 tablespoons of olive oil; sauté for 3 minutes. To the saucepan, add the drained pasta, vegetables, oregano, tomatoes, pasta sauce, feta cheese, pepper, red pepper flakes and remaining ¼ teaspoon salt; toss well. Transfer mixture to individual ramekins and sprinkle mozzarella cheese on top. Cover and bake for 20 minutes. Uncover and bake 10 additional minutes or until cooked through.

This may also be baked in a covered 9 x 13″ baking dish for 30 minutes and then continue baking uncovered for an additional 20 minutes. Serve as a main dish in individual bowls.

Salmon and Artichoke Pasta Blend

Makes 4 to 6 servings

Ingredients

8 oz. uncooked angel hair
or vermicelli pasta, broken
in thirds

1½ C. fresh cauliflower
or broccoli florets

½ C. chopped celery

⅓ C. finely chopped red onion

1 (2.25 oz.) can sliced
black olives

1 (7 oz.) jar marinated
artichoke hearts, drained
and coarsely chopped

½ C. sliced water chestnuts,
optional

3 T. chopped basil or cilantro
leaves or to taste

2 T. chopped parsley or to taste

½ tsp. garlic salt

¼ tsp. celery seeds

¼ tsp. pepper

½ C. mayonnaise

1 lb. salmon fillets, cooked,
flaked and chilled

Spring greens, optional

Directions

In a large saucepan over medium-high heat, bring lightly salted water to a boil. Add pasta to water, stir and return to a boil. Cook uncovered for 5 to 6 minutes or to desired doneness, stirring occasionally. Drain pasta in a colander and rinse with cold water to cool quickly. Place pasta in a large bowl. Add cauliflower, celery, red onion, olives, artichokes, water chestnuts, basil, parsley, garlic salt, celery seeds, pepper and mayonnaise. Toss gently to coat completely. Fold in the salmon. Line individual serving bowls with spring greens, if desired, and serve pasta on top.

Spicy Ham-Apple Pasta Salad

Makes 4 servings

Ingredients

2 C. uncooked bow tie pasta

2 C. cubed cooked ham

2 unpeeled apples, cored and sliced

1 C. pineapple preserves

1 C. apple jelly

⅓ C. prepared horseradish or to taste

1½ tsp. dry mustard

1 tsp. pepper

Lettuce leaves

Directions

In a large saucepan over medium-high heat, bring lightly salted water to a boil. Add pasta to water, stir and return to a boil. Cook uncovered for 10 to 13 minutes or to desired doneness, stirring occasionally. Drain pasta in a colander and rinse with cold water to cool quickly. Transfer pasta to a large bowl. Stir in ham and apples and set aside. In a small bowl, whisk together the preserves, jelly, horseradish, dry mustard and pepper until well blended. Pour mixture over the pasta mixture in bowl and toss to combine. Cover bowl and refrigerate for 30 minutes. Before serving, place a few lettuce leaves in individual serving bowls and arrange ham salad on top.

Calypso Crabmeat Pasta

Makes 4 servings

Ingredients

3 C. uncooked rotini pasta

1 (8 oz.) pkg. imitation crabmeat, flaked

1 red bell pepper, thinly sliced

1 mango, peeled, seeded and cubed

2 T. chopped fresh cilantro

1 jalapeno pepper*, seeded and minced

1 tsp. grated lime peel

3 T. fresh lime juice

2 T. extra-virgin olive oil

1 T. honey

½ tsp. ground cumin

½ tsp. ground ginger

¼ tsp. salt

Directions

In a large saucepan over medium-high heat, bring lightly salted water to a boil. Add pasta to water, stir and return to a boil. Cook uncovered for 8 to 10 minutes or to desired doneness, stirring occasionally. Drain pasta in a colander and rinse with cold water to cool quickly. Transfer cooled pasta to a large bowl. Add crabmeat, red pepper, mango, cilantro and jalapeno pepper; mix and set aside. In a small bowl, whisk together lime peel, lime juice, olive oil, honey, cumin, ginger and salt until well blended. Pour dressing over pasta and toss to coat well. Cover bowl and refrigerate for at least one hour before serving.

Wear gloves when working with jalapeno peppers to avoid burns caused by contact with skin and eyes.

Potluck Spaghetti Salad

Makes 15 servings

Ingredients

12 oz. uncooked thin spaghetti

1 C. shredded mozzarella cheese

½ C. diced pepperoni

½ C. diced fully cooked ham

½ C. seeded and chopped green bell pepper

½ C. diced tomato

½ C. chopped onion

¼ C. sliced black olives

½ C. seeded and chopped cucumber, optional

1 avocado, peeled, pitted and diced, optional

1 (8 oz.) bottle Italian salad dressing

Directions

In a large saucepan over medium-high heat, bring lightly salted water a boil. Add pasta to water, stir and return to a boil. Cook uncovered for 8 to 10 minutes or to desired doneness, stirring occasionally. Meanwhile, in a large bowl, combine the cheese, pepperoni, ham, green pepper, tomato, onion, olives, optional cucumber and optional avocado. Drain pasta in a colander and rinse with cold water to cool quickly. Drain well and add spaghetti to the ingredients in the bowl. Drizzle desired amount of salad dressing on top and toss lightly to coat all ingredients well. Cover bowl and refrigerate salad until chilled.

Hearty Antipasto

Makes 10 to 12 servings

Ingredients

3 C. uncooked tricolor
spiral pasta

4 oz. provolone cheese, cubed

4 oz. Monterey Jack
cheese, cubed

4 oz. sliced pepperoni,
quartered

4 oz. hard salami, cubed

1 medium green bell pepper,
seeded and diced

2 stalks celery, chopped

1 small onion, chopped

2 plum tomatoes, sliced
and halved

1 (2.25 oz.) can sliced black
olives, drained

1 to 2 T. minced fresh
chives, optional

⅓ C. extra-virgin olive oil
or vegetable oil

¼ C. apple cider vinegar

1½ tsp. dried oregano

¾ tsp. salt

½ tsp. pepper

Directions

In a large saucepan over medium-high heat, bring lightly salted water to a boil. Add pasta to water, stir and return to a boil. Cook uncovered for 8 to 10 minutes or to desired doneness, stirring occasionally. Drain pasta in a colander and rinse with cold water to cool quickly. In a large bowl, combine the pasta, provolone cheese, Monterey Jack cheese, pepperoni, salami, green pepper, celery, onion, tomatoes, olives and optional chives; set aside. In a jar with a tight-fitting lid, combine the oil, vinegar, oregano, salt and pepper. Cover and shake well until dressing is thoroughly blended. Pour dressing over pasta mixture and toss to coat all ingredients. Cover bowl and chill well before serving.

Mediterranean Chicken Pasta

Makes 4 servings

Ingredients

6 T. extra-virgin olive oil

2 T. plus 2 tsp. tarragon
  vinegar

1 T. chopped fresh tarragon

1½ tsp. fresh lemon juice

1½ tsp. Dijon mustard

Salt and pepper

3 C. diced cooked chicken

½ C. uncooked orzo pasta

1 C. halved cherry tomatoes

1 (6 oz.) jar marinated
  artichoke hearts, drained

½ C. pitted and coarsely
  chopped Kalamata olives

⅓ C. golden raisins

1½ T. drained capers

Directions

In a small bowl, whisk together oil, vinegar, tarragon, lemon juice and mustard until well blended. Season with salt and pepper to taste. In a medium bowl, combine chicken and ¼ cup of the dressing. Stir to coat well and set aside. In a large saucepan over medium-high heat, bring lightly salted water to a boil. Add pasta to water, stir and return to a boil. Cook uncovered for 5 to 8 minutes or to desired doneness, stirring occasionally. Drain pasta in a colander and rinse with cold water to cool quickly. Transfer pasta to a large bowl and stir in remaining dressing, tossing to coat well. Add chicken mixture, tomatoes, artichokes, olives, raisins and capers; mix well. Season with additional salt and pepper to taste. Serve immediately.

Hawaiian Chicken Salad

Makes 10 to 12 servings

Ingredients

3 C. uncooked medium
  pasta shells

1 tsp. extra-virgin olive oil

1 C. frozen baby peas

1 C. mayonnaise

1 C. creamy salad dressing

3 C. cooked, diced chicken

1 (8 oz.) can crushed
  pineapple, drained

½ C. chopped red onion

1 C. chopped celery

Salt and pepper

1 (11 oz.) can mandarin
  oranges, drained

1 C. chopped salted cashews

½ C. flaked coconut, optional

Directions

In a large saucepan over medium-high heat, bring lightly salted water to a boil. Add pasta to water, stir and return to a boil. Cook uncovered for 9 to 12 minutes or to desired doneness, stirring occasionally. Drain pasta in a colander and return pasta to pan. Toss with olive oil and stir in frozen peas; cover pan and let it rest for 5 minutes. In a large bowl, combine mayonnaise and salad dressing; mix well. Add pasta mixture, chicken, pineapple, red onion and celery, stirring to coat well. Season with salt and pepper to taste. Gently fold in mandarin oranges. Transfer mixture to a serving bowl, cover and refrigerate overnight. Before serving, top with cashews; sprinkle with coconut, if desired.

Crab and Veggie Pasta

Makes 6 servings

Ingredients

1 head fresh broccoli, cut into florets

1 head fresh cauliflower, broken into small florets

2 tomatoes, chopped

½ C. chopped fresh chives

1 (8 oz.) pkg. imitation crabmeat

12 oz. uncooked tri-color spiral pasta

2 C. balsamic vinaigrette or Italian salad dressing

Directions

In a large bowl, combine broccoli, cauliflower, tomatoes, chives and crabmeat; stir well and set aside. In a large saucepan over medium-high heat, bring lightly salted water to a boil. Add pasta to water, stir and return to a boil. Cook uncovered for 8 to 10 minutes or to desired doneness, stirring occasionally. Drain pasta in a colander and rinse with cold water to cool quickly. Add pasta to the crabmeat mixture and toss. Pour desired amount of salad dressing over mixture in bowl and toss to coat ingredients. Cover bowl and chill well before serving.

Bistro-Style Pasta Chicken with Parmesan

Makes 4 servings

Ingredients

1 C. uncooked penne or rotini pasta

2 skinless boneless chicken breast halves, grilled

1 C. quartered cherry tomatoes

¼ C. chopped red onion

¼ C. drained and chopped sun-dried tomatoes

⅓ C. lightly packed fresh basil leaves, cut into strips

1 C. shredded Parmesan cheese

½ C. Caesar or Italian salad dressing

Directions

In a large saucepan over medium-high heat, bring lightly salted water to a boil. Add pasta to water, stir and return to a boil. Cook uncovered for 8 to 10 minutes or to desired doneness, stirring occasionally. Drain pasta in a colander and rinse with cold water to cool quickly. Cut grilled chicken breasts into ¼″ strips. In a large bowl, combine pasta, chicken strips, cherry tomatoes, red onion, sun-dried tomatoes, basil and Parmesan cheese. Pour salad dressing over mixture in bowl and toss to coat ingredients. Serve immediately or chill in refrigerator before serving.

To serve this salad warm, omit cold water rinsing of pasta and combine the warm pasta and warm chicken strips with other ingredients just before serving.

Poppy Seed Chicken and Bow Ties

Makes 6 to 8 servings

Ingredients

12 oz. uncooked bow tie pasta

2 C. chopped grilled chicken

1 (6 oz.) pkg. sweetened dried cranberries

½ C. finely chopped celery

¼ C. chopped green onions

3 oz. slivered almonds

½ C. prepared poppy seed salad dressing

1 tsp. garlic salt

Salt and pepper

Directions

In a large saucepan over medium-high heat, bring lightly salted water to a boil. Add pasta to water, stir and return to a boil. Cook uncovered for 10 to 13 minutes or to desired doneness, stirring occasionally. Drain pasta in a colander and rinse with cold water to cool quickly. In a large bowl, combine cooled pasta, chicken, dried cranberries, celery, green onions and almonds. Stir in the dressing and garlic salt. Season with salt and pepper to taste, tossing to coat well. Cover and refrigerate until chilled.

For a creamier dressing, blend ½ cup plain yogurt with poppy seed dressing before adding to salad.

Shrimp and Pasta Combo

Makes 6 servings

Ingredients

10 oz. uncooked penne
or elbow macaroni pasta

2 (5 oz.) pkgs. precooked
frozen shrimp, thawed

½ C. low-fat Caesar dressing

2 tsp. minced sun-dried
tomatoes

¾ C. thinly sliced cucumber

⅓ C. chopped fresh basil

¼ C. pitted and chopped
Kalamata olives

½ small red onion, sliced
into rings

1 (7 oz.) bottle roasted red bell
peppers, drained and cut
into strips

¾ C. crumbled feta cheese

¼ tsp. pepper

Chopped fresh parsley,
optional

Directions

In a large saucepan over medium-high heat, bring lightly salted water to a boil. Add pasta to water, stir and return to a boil. Cook uncovered for 8 to 10 minutes or to desired doneness, stirring occasionally. Drain pasta in a colander and rinse with cold water to cool quickly. Rinse thawed shrimp in cold water; drain well. In a large bowl, combine shrimp, cooled pasta, dressing, tomatoes, cucumber, basil, Kalamata olives, red onion and red peppers; toss gently to coat. Cover and refrigerate for 1 hour or until chilled. Just before serving, sprinkle cheese and pepper on top. Garnish with parsley, if desired.

Super Pasta Pointer

Pasta Term: Orecchiette
Meaning "little ears", this type of pasta is shaped like its name.

Tomato-Mozzarella
Pasta Blend

Makes 6 to 8 servings

Ingredients

¼ C. red wine vinegar

1 clove garlic, minced

½ tsp. salt

Pepper

⅔ C. extra-virgin olive oil

1 pt. cherry tomatoes, halved

1½ C. cubed mozzarella cheese

¼ C. chopped onion

3 T. minced fresh basil

2 C. uncooked bow tie pasta

15 pitted black olives

Directions

In a small bowl, combine vinegar, garlic, salt and pepper to taste. Whisk in oil until well blended; set aside. In a medium bowl, combine tomatoes, cheese, onion and basil. Add dressing and toss to coat well; set aside. In a large saucepan over medium-high heat, bring lightly salted water to a boil. Add pasta to water, stir and return to a boil. Cook uncovered for 10 to 13 minutes or to desired doneness, stirring occasionally. Drain pasta in a colander and rinse with cold water to cool quickly. Add pasta and olives to the other ingredients and toss well to coat. Cover and refrigerate for at least 1 hour, stirring occasionally. Serve in a glass bowl with a slotted spoon.

Mediterranean Pasta and Vegetables

Makes 4 to 6 servings

Ingredients

1⅓ C. uncooked rotini pasta

1 medium zucchini,
   thinly sliced

1 medium carrot, thinly sliced

1 small green bell pepper,
   seeded and chopped

1 small red bell pepper, seeded
   and chopped

1 (2.25 oz.) can sliced black
   olives, drained

½ C. crumbled feta cheese

½ tsp. crushed red
   pepper flakes

1 C. zesty Italian
   salad dressing

Fresh mint leaves, optional

Directions

In a large saucepan over medium-high heat, bring lightly salted water to a boil. Add pasta to water, stir and return to a boil. Cook uncovered for 8 to 10 minutes or to desired doneness, stirring occasionally. Drain pasta in a colander and rinse with cold water to cool quickly. In a large bowl, combine cooked pasta, zucchini, carrot, green pepper, red pepper, black olives, feta cheese and red pepper flakes. Drizzle dressing on salad and toss to coat well. Cover and refrigerate for 1 hour or until ready to serve. Just before serving, garnish with fresh mint leaves, if desired.

Thai Noodles and Veggie Salad

Makes 6 to 8 servings

Ingredients

8 oz. uncooked Udon noodles

½ C. unsalted crunchy
peanut butter

½ C. milk

1 tsp. grated fresh gingerroot

1 clove garlic, minced

3 T. rice wine vinegar

3 T. soy sauce

1 T. dark sesame oil

⅛ tsp. crushed red
pepper flakes

1 cucumber, peeled, seeded
and thinly sliced

2 C. fresh bean sprouts

2 carrots, peeled and grated

6 green onions, thinly sliced

¼ C. chopped fresh mint

1 head romaine lettuce, torn

1 C. chopped peanuts

Directions

In a large saucepan over medium-high heat, bring lightly salted water to a boil. Add pasta to water, stir and return to a boil. Cook uncovered for about 5 minutes or to desired doneness, stirring occasionally. Drain pasta in a colander and rinse with cold water to cool quickly. In a small bowl, whisk together the peanut butter, milk, ginger, garlic, vinegar, soy sauce, sesame oil and red pepper flakes until well blended. In a large bowl, combine the cooked noodles, cucumber, bean sprouts, carrots, green onions and mint. Whisk the peanut butter dressing and pour it over the salad; stir together until well coated. Cover bowl and refrigerate until chilled. Place portions of lettuce into individual serving bowls and spoon chilled pasta salad on top. Garnish with the chopped peanuts.

Super Pasta Pointer

Udon (oo DOAN) noodles are like thick spaghetti in different widths and can be found in Asian grocery or health food stores. Whole wheat spaghetti or linguine can be substituted.

Minestrone Macaroni Salad

Makes 4 servings

Ingredients

½ C. uncooked elbow
macaroni pasta

1 large tomato, chopped

1 (15 oz.) can garbanzo beans,
rinsed and drained

2 stalks celery, chopped

¼ C. shredded Parmesan
cheese

2 T. bottled Italian salad
dressing

Salt and pepper

Directions

In a medium saucepan over medium-high heat, bring lightly salted water to a boil. Add pasta to water, stir and return to a boil. Cook uncovered for 7 to 10 minutes or to desired doneness, stirring occasionally. Drain pasta in a colander and rinse with cold water to cool quickly. Transfer macaroni to a medium salad bowl. Add tomato, beans, celery and cheese; toss well. Add salad dressing and toss again to coat. Season with salt and pepper to taste and serve immediately.

Super Pasta Pointer

Pasta Term: Cappelletti
*Small stuffed circles of pasta that resemble "little hats",
which is what this Italian word means.*

Ricotta-Topped Twists

Makes 6 servings

Ingredients

8 oz. uncooked gemelli
   or other spiral pasta

10 sun-dried tomatoes in
   oil, drained

1 T. red wine vinegar

2 tsp. salt-packed capers, rinsed

2 cloves garlic, minced

½ C. extra-virgin olive oil

Salt and pepper

½ C. grape or cherry
   tomatoes, quartered

⅓ C. pitted, halved
   Kalamata olives

⅓ C. torn fresh basil

Ricotta cheese

Extra-virgin olive
   oil, optional

Directions

In a medium saucepan over medium-high heat, bring lightly salted water to a boil. Add pasta to water, stir and return to a boil. Cook uncovered for 10 to 13 minutes or to desired doneness, stirring occasionally. Meanwhile, in a food processor, combine tomatoes, vinegar, capers and garlic; pulse to blend. With machine running, slowly add ½ cup oil and process until mixture is smooth. Season with salt and pepper. Drain cooked pasta in a colander and rinse with cold water to cool quickly. Transfer pasta to a large bowl and add tomato mixture, grape tomatoes, olives and basil; toss to mix well. Place portions of pasta mixture in individual serving bowls and top with a small scoop of ricotta cheese. Drizzle with a little oil and sprinkle with additional pepper, if desired.

Creamy Tortellini and Peas

Makes 5 servings

Ingredients

¼ C. reduced-fat mayonnaise

¼ C. sour cream

2 T. prepared basil pesto

1 T. chopped fresh mint leaves

½ tsp. salt

⅛ tsp. pepper

1 (9 oz.) pkg. refrigerated
cheese-filled tortellini,
uncooked

2 C. frozen baby peas,
slightly thawed

1 C. cubed mozzarella cheese

2 green onions, thinly sliced

Fresh mint leaves, optional

Directions

In a small bowl, combine mayonnaise, sour cream, pesto, mint, salt and pepper; mix until well blended. Cover and refrigerate. In a large saucepan over medium-high heat, bring lightly salted water to a boil. Add pasta to water, stir and return to a boil. Cook uncovered for 8 to 10 minutes or to desired doneness, stirring occasionally. Drain tortellini in a colander and rinse once with cold water to cool slightly. In a large bowl, combine warm tortellini and peas; let mixture rest for 5 minutes. Add cheese and green onions. Pour mayonnaise mixture over salad and toss to coat lightly. Cover and refrigerate for at least 1 hour. Before serving, garnish with fresh mint leaves, if desired.

Squash and Walnut Pesto Shells

Makes 4 to 6 servings

Ingredients

2½ C. peeled, cubed
  butternut squash

¾ tsp. salt, divided

½ C. fresh flat-leaf parsley

2½ T. chopped walnuts

2 T. fresh sage leaves

2 T. lemon juice

2 T. extra-virgin olive oil

1 clove garlic, chopped

⅓ C. low-sodium
  chicken broth

6 oz. uncooked medium shell
  or corkscrew pasta

4 C. torn baby spinach
  or arugula

¼ C. thinly sliced green onions

½ tsp. pepper

Grated Parmesan cheese,
  optional

Directions

Preheat oven to 450°. Lightly coat a jelly roll pan with nonstick cooking spray. Arrange squash pieces in a single layer on pan and spray squash with cooking spray. Sprinkle ¼ teaspoon salt evenly over squash. Bake for 20 minutes or until squash is tender, stirring after 10 minutes. Cool squash slightly. Meanwhile, in a large saucepan over medium-high heat, bring lightly salted water to a boil. Add pasta to water, stir and return to a boil. Cook uncovered for 9 to 12 minutes or to desired doneness, stirring occasionally. In a food processor, combine ¼ teaspoon salt, parsley, walnuts, sage, lemon juice, oil and garlic. Process until ingredients are finely chopped, scraping sides as needed. With processor running, slowly add broth and process until pesto is well blended. Drain cooked pasta in a colander and rinse with cold water to cool quickly. In a large bowl, mix the pasta, squash, remaining ¼ teaspoon salt and blended pesto, tossing well to coat. Add the spinach, green onions and pepper; toss to combine and serve immediately.

Tasty Tarragon Pasta Toss

Makes 4 servings

Ingredients

8 oz. uncooked pasta al ceppo
or penne pasta

1 red bell pepper, seeded
and cut into strips

½ C. chopped red onion

2 C. sliced and quartered
zucchini pieces

16 Kalamata or black
olives, pitted

1 C. baby spinach leaves, torn

3 T. extra-virgin olive oil

2 T. tarragon vinegar

1 tsp. sugar

½ tsp. salt

½ tsp. white pepper

2 cloves garlic, minced

Fresh thyme sprigs, optional

Directions

In a large saucepan over medium-high heat, bring lightly salted water to a boil. Add pasta to water, stir and return to a boil. Cook uncovered for 12 to 15 minutes or to desired doneness, stirring occasionally. Meanwhile, in a large bowl, combine red pepper, red onion, zucchini, olives and spinach; set aside. In a small bowl, whisk together oil, vinegar, sugar, salt, white pepper and garlic. Drain cooked pasta in a colander and rinse with cold water to cool quickly. Add pasta to the vegetables in the bowl. Drizzle tarragon dressing over top and toss to coat. Garnish with a few sprigs of fresh thyme, if desired. Salad can be served immediately or refrigerated for several hours.

Super Pasta Pointer

Pasta al ceppo (PAH stah al CHAY poh) is the Italian phrase for "pasta on a stick". Originally, the dough was wrapped around knitting needles to create long rolled tubes of pasta. Penne or mostaccioli pasta can be substituted.

Savory Italian Pasta Combo

Makes 12 servings, approximately 200 calories per ¾-cup serving

Ingredients

2 (14.5 oz.) cans stewed
  tomatoes

2 C. fresh broccoli florets

2 medium carrots,
  thinly sliced

½ tsp. salt

½ tsp. Italian seasoning

½ tsp. dried oregano

¼ tsp. dried basil

4 strips bacon, diced

½ lb. fresh mushrooms, sliced

⅓ C. chopped green bell pepper

¼ C. chopped onion

2 cloves garlic, minced

12 oz. uncooked medium
  shell pasta

¼ C. shredded Parmesan
  cheese

Directions

In a large saucepan over medium heat, combine tomatoes, broccoli, carrots, salt, Italian seasoning, oregano and basil; bring mixture to a boil. Reduce heat, cover and simmer for 25 to 30 minutes or until broccoli and carrots are tender. Meanwhile, cook bacon until crisp in a large skillet over medium heat. Transfer bacon to paper towels to drain, reserving 1 tablespoon of drippings in pan. Add mushrooms, green pepper, onion and garlic to pan and sauté until tender. Add mushroom mixture to tomato mixture in saucepan and heat through. In a large saucepan over medium-high heat, bring lightly salted water to a boil. Add pasta to water, stir and return to a boil. Cook uncovered for 10 to 13 minutes or to desired doneness, stirring occasionally. Drain pasta and place in a large serving bowl; top with vegetable mixture, then sprinkle with bacon and Parmesan cheese. Serve immediately.

Orange Poppy
Seed Linguine

Makes 4 servings, approximately 130 calories per ¾-cup serving

Ingredients

6 oz. uncooked linguine pasta

2 T. butter

½ tsp. finely shredded
   orange peel

¼ C. orange juice

2 tsp. poppy seeds

Directions

In a large saucepan over medium-high heat, bring lightly salted water to a boil. Add pasta to water, stir and return to a boil. Cook uncovered for 9 to 12 minutes or to desired doneness, stirring occasionally. Drain in a colander and transfer to a medium bowl. Add butter, orange peel, orange juice and poppy seeds, tossing lightly until butter melts. Serve immediately.

Super Pasta Pointer

Meal Planning for Pasta Lovers with Hearty Appetites
Use 2 to 3 oz. of uncooked pasta for each serving of a pasta main dish. Use about 2 oz. of uncooked pasta for each serving of a pasta side dish. Use 1½ to 2 oz. of uncooked pasta for each serving of a pasta appetizer.

Crowd-Pleasing Slow Cooker Spaghetti Sauce

*Makes 20 servings, approximately 250 calories per
1-cup serving of spaghetti with ½ cup sauce
topped with 1 tablespoon of Parmesan cheese*

Ingredients

5 (29 oz.) cans tomato sauce

3 (6 oz.) cans tomato paste

3 cloves garlic, minced

1 medium onion, chopped

1 T. dried rosemary

1 T. dried oregano

1 T. dried thyme or basil

1 T. dried parsley

1 bay leaf

1 T. brown sugar

⅛ tsp. crushed red
  pepper flakes

Salt and pepper

Uncooked spaghetti
  or other pasta

Grated Parmesan cheese

Directions

In a 6-quart slow cooker, combine tomato sauce, tomato paste, garlic, onion, rosemary, oregano, thyme, parsley, bay leaf, brown sugar, red pepper flakes, salt and pepper to taste. Stir until well blended. Cook on high for 3 to 4 hours, stirring frequently. Shortly before mealtime, bring lightly salted water to a boil in a large saucepan over medium-high heat. Add desired amount of pasta to water, stir and return to a boil. Cook uncovered for 8 to 10 minutes or to desired doneness, stirring occasionally. Drain pasta in a colander and transfer to a large serving bowl. Serve immediately with spaghetti sauce and Parmesan cheese sprinkled on top.

Super Pasta Pointer

If you are not serving a whole crowd, freeze leftover sauce in small containers for use later in combination dishes, such as lasagna, or over any type of cooked pasta.

Bow Ties with
Red Pepper Sauce

Makes 4 servings, approximately 140 calories per 1-cup serving

Ingredients

2 C. seeded and chopped red
   bell pepper

½ C. chicken broth

1 T. chopped fresh oregano

¼ tsp. salt

¼ tsp. pepper

1 T. tomato paste

1 T. balsamic vinegar

1 tsp. honey

2 C. uncooked bow tie pasta

1 C. frozen green peas,
   blanched and cooled

1 T. chopped fresh parsley

Directions

In a medium saucepan over medium-low heat, combine bell pepper, broth, oregano, salt and pepper. Cook mixture for 20 minutes, stirring occasionally, until red pepper is tender. Stir in tomato paste, vinegar and honey; remove from heat. In a blender or food processor, puree the mixture until smooth. Meanwhile, in a large saucepan over medium-high heat, bring lightly salted water to a boil. Add pasta to water, stir and return to a boil. Cook uncovered for 10 to 13 minutes or to desired doneness, stirring occasionally. Drain cooked pasta and transfer to a large bowl. Add red pepper sauce, peas and parsley; stir to combine and serve immediately.

Southwestern Black Bean Pasta

Makes 6 servings, approximately 250 calories per 1-cup serving

Ingredients

8 oz. uncooked gemelli or other spiral or corkscrew pasta

1 C. finely chopped green pepper

1 medium onion, chopped

2 cloves garlic, minced

1 tsp. dried oregano

½ tsp. ground cumin

½ tsp. crushed red pepper flakes or 1 dash of chili powder

2 C. tomato sauce

1 (15 oz.) can black beans, rinsed and drained

2 T. canned diced green chiles, optional

½ C. shredded reduced-fat Cheddar cheese

Directions

In a large saucepan over medium-high heat, bring lightly salted water to a boil. Add pasta to water, stir and return to a boil. Cook uncovered for 10 to 13 minutes or to desired doneness, stirring occasionally. Meanwhile, in a large saucepan coated with nonstick cooking spray, combine the green pepper, onion, garlic, oregano, cumin and red pepper flakes. Cook over medium heat for 5 minutes or until vegetables are tender. Add tomato sauce, black beans and optional green chiles; reduce heat and simmer uncovered for 5 minutes or until heated through. Drain cooked pasta and add it to saucepan; stir to mix. Transfer mixture to a serving bowl and sprinkle with cheese. Serve immediately.

Angel Hair Summer Salad

Makes 8 servings, approximately 120 calories per ¾-cup serving

Ingredients

7 oz. uncooked angel
hair pasta

4 plum tomatoes, seeded
and chopped

1 C. thinly sliced carrot
rounds

1 medium cucumber,
chopped

6 green onions, thinly sliced

2 T. extra-virgin olive oil

2 T. apple cider vinegar

½ tsp. salt

¼ tsp. pepper

Directions

In a large saucepan over medium-high heat, bring lightly salted water to a boil. Add pasta to water, stir and return to a boil. Cook uncovered for 5 to 6 minutes or to desired doneness, stirring occasionally. Drain pasta in a colander and rinse with cold water to cool quickly. Transfer pasta to a large bowl. Add tomatoes, carrots, cucumber and green onions; stir to mix well. In a small bowl, whisk together the oil, vinegar, salt and pepper. Pour dressing over pasta mixture and toss to coat. Cover and refrigerate for 4 hours. Serve chilled.

Super Pasta Pointer

Pasta Term: Acini de pepe
The Italian word for "peppercorns", this pasta is shaped like tiny beads.

Turkey, Ham and Blue Cheese Blend

Makes 6 to 7 servings, approximately 220 calories per 1-cup serving

Ingredients

1½ C. uncooked small shell pasta

1 C. cubed cooked turkey or chicken breast

1 C. cubed cooked ham

1 to 2 oz. blue cheese, crumbled

¼ C. chopped pimiento

¼ C. chopped onion

½ C. diced celery

¼ C. coarsely shredded carrot

¼ C. diced zucchini

½ C. sour cream

¼ C. low-calorie mayonnaise

White pepper

Directions

In a large saucepan over medium-high heat, bring lightly salted water to a boil. Add pasta to water, stir and return to a boil. Cook uncovered for 8 to 10 minutes or to desired doneness, stirring occasionally. Drain pasta in a colander and rinse with cold water to cool quickly. In a large bowl, combine turkey, ham, blue cheese, pimiento, onion, celery, carrot and zucchini; mix well. In a small bowl, mix sour cream and mayonnaise; pour over mixture in bowl and stir. Add pasta and toss well. Season with white pepper to taste. Transfer mixture to a serving bowl, cover and refrigerate for at least 2 hours before serving.

Chilled Seafood and Bow Tie Toss

Makes 10 servings, approximately 220 calories per 1-cup serving

Ingredients

16 oz. uncooked bowtie pasta

½ lb. imitation crabmeat, chopped

⅓ lb. precooked frozen salad shrimp, thawed

1 or 2 stalks celery, chopped

⅓ C. finely chopped green onions

¼ C. diced green pepper

1⅓ C. fat-free mayonnaise

4 tsp. dill pickle relish

4 tsp. Dijon mustard

1 tsp. salt

1 tsp. dried dillweed

¼ tsp. pepper

Directions

In a large saucepan over medium-high heat, bring lightly salted water to a boil. Add pasta to water, stir and return to a boil. Cook uncovered for 10 to 13 minutes or to desired doneness, stirring occasionally. Drain pasta in a colander and rinse with cold water to cool quickly. Place pasta in a large bowl. Add crabmeat, shrimp, celery, green onions and green pepper. In another bowl, whisk together mayonnaise, pickle relish, mustard, salt, dillweed and pepper. Pour over pasta mixture and toss to coat. Cover and refrigerate pasta for at least 2 hours before serving.

Pasta de Santa Fe

Makes 8 servings, approximately 300 calories per 1-cup serving

Ingredients

16 oz. uncooked rotini
  or other spiral pasta

1¼ C. tomato juice

1½ T. extra-virgin olive oil

1 T. red wine vinegar

1½ tsp. chili powder

¾ tsp. paprika

½ tsp. salt

¼ tsp. pepper

½ C. grated Parmesan cheese

½ C. whole corn kernels,
  cooked and cooled

⅓ C. chopped fresh cilantro

¼ C. chopped green onions

2 T. diced red bell pepper

2 T. diced green bell pepper

1 skinless boneless chicken
  breast half, cooked
  and diced

Directions

In a large saucepan over medium-high heat, bring lightly salted water to a boil. Add pasta to water, stir and return to a boil. Cook uncovered for 8 to 10 minutes or to desired doneness, stirring occasionally. Drain pasta in a colander and rinse with cold water to cool quickly. Transfer pasta to a large bowl. In a small bowl, combine tomato juice, olive oil, vinegar, chili powder, paprika, salt and pepper; whisk until well blended. Pour dressing over pasta in bowl, mix well, cover and refrigerate for 2 to 4 hours. In a medium bowl, combine the Parmesan cheese, corn kernels, cilantro, green onions, red pepper, green pepper and diced chicken breast. Add to chilled pasta mixture, stir, cover and refrigerate for 8 hours or overnight before serving.

Quick-Fix Summer Pasta

Makes 5 servings, approximately 120 calories per ¾-cup serving

Ingredients

1½ C. uncooked tri-color spiral pasta

1 (8 oz.) can unsweetened pineapple chunks with juice

1 C. halved fresh snow peas

½ C. thinly sliced carrot

½ C. sliced cucumber, peeled and seeded

1 T. minced fresh cilantro

¼ C. bottled fat-free Italian salad dressing

Directions

In a large saucepan over medium-high heat, bring lightly salted water to a boil. Add pasta to water, stir and return to a boil. Cook uncovered for 8 to 10 minutes or to desired doneness, stirring occasionally. Meanwhile, drain pineapple, reserving ¼ cup juice. In a large bowl, combine the pineapple, snow peas, carrot, cucumber and reserved pineapple juice. Drain pasta in a colander and rinse with cold water to cool quickly. Add pasta to pineapple mixture. Sprinkle with cilantro. Drizzle with salad dressing and toss to coat. Chill until serving.

Confetti Pasta Chill

Makes 8 to 10 servings, approximately 135 calories per ¾-cup serving

Ingredients

1½ C. uncooked tri-color
spiral pasta

1 (16 oz.) pkg. frozen corn
kernels, thawed

1 C. chopped celery

1 medium green bell
pepper, chopped

1 C. chopped, seeded tomatoes

½ C. diced pimientos

½ C. chopped red onion

1 C. picante sauce

2 T. vegetable oil

1 T. lemon juice

1 clove garlic, minced

1 T. sugar

½ tsp. salt

Directions

In a large saucepan over medium-high heat, bring lightly salted water to a boil. Add pasta to water, stir and return to a boil. Cook uncovered for 8 to 10 minutes or to desired doneness, stirring occasionally. Drain pasta in a colander and rinse with cold water to cool quickly. In a large bowl, combine the pasta, corn, celery, green pepper, tomatoes, pimientos and red onion. In a jar with a tight-fitting lid, combine the picante sauce, oil, lemon juice, garlic, sugar and salt. Cover jar and shake until well blended. Pour dressing over pasta mixture and toss to coat well. Cover bowl and refrigerate overnight. Serve chilled.

Tuna Toss

Makes 4 servings, approximately 270 calories per 1-cup serving

Ingredients

6 oz. whole-wheat penne pasta

1 (7 oz.) jar roasted red
   peppers, divided

1 (6 oz.) can chunk light
   tuna in water, drained

½ C. finely chopped
   red onion

2 T. capers, rinsed
   and chopped

2 T. non-fat plain yogurt

2 T. chopped fresh basil

1 T. extra-virgin olive oil

1½ tsp. lemon juice

1 clove garlic, minced

⅛ tsp. salt

Pepper

Directions

In a large saucepan over medium-high heat, bring lightly salted water to a boil. Add pasta to water, stir and return to a boil. Cook uncovered for 10 to 13 minutes or to desired doneness, stirring occasionally. Meanwhile, rinse and slice the roasted red peppers; set aside. In a large bowl, combine tuna, ⅓ cup red peppers, red onion and capers; set aside. In a blender or food processor, combine yogurt, basil, oil, lemon juice, garlic, salt, pepper and remaining red peppers. Puree until mixture is smooth. Drain cooked pasta in a colander and rinse with cold water to cool quickly. Add pasta to tuna mixture. Pour red pepper sauce over mixture and toss to coat.

Index

Warm and Wonderful

Cool and Classy

On the Lighter Side

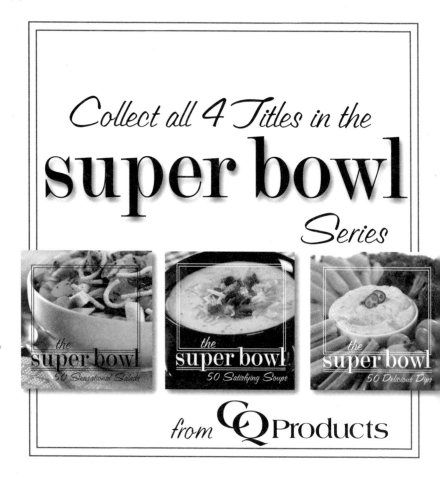

Collect all *4 Titles* in the

super bowl

Series

the super bowl
50 Sensational Salads

the super bowl
50 Satisfying Soups

the super bowl
50 Delicious Dips

from CQ Products